SportsZone Biographies

PATRICK MAHOMES

BY Anthony K. Hewson

SportsZone

An Imprint of Abdo Publishing
abdobooks.com

abdobooks.com

Published by Abdo Publishing, a division of ABDO, PO Box 398166, Minneapolis, Minnesota 55439. Copyright © 2024 by Abdo Consulting Group, Inc. International copyrights reserved in all countries. No part of this book may be reproduced in any form without written permission from the publisher. SportsZone™ is a trademark and logo of Abdo Publishing.

Printed in the United States of America, North Mankato, Minnesota.
052023
092023

THIS BOOK CONTAINS
RECYCLED MATERIALS

Cover Photos: Michael Reaves/Getty Images Sport/Getty Images
Interior Photos: Christian Petersen/Getty Images Sport/Getty Images, 5; Kathy Willens/ AP Images, 7; Mo Khursheed/TFV Media/AP Images, 9; Jamie Squire/Getty Images Sport/Getty Images, 11; Travis Heying/AP Images, 13; Wilfredo Lee/AP Images, 15; Logan Bowles/AP Images, 17; Dustin Bradford/Getty Images Sport/Getty Images, 18; Tom Pennington/Getty Images Sport/Getty Images, 21; Kevin C. Cox/Getty Images Sport/ Getty Images, 22; David Eulitt/Getty Images Sport/Getty Images, 25; Ashley Landis/AP Images, 27; Adam Hunger/AP Images, 29

Editors: Charlie Beattie and Steph Giedd
Series Designer: Karli Kruse

LIBRARY OF CONGRESS CONTROL NUMBER: 2022949134

Publisher's Cataloging-in-Publication Data

Names: Hewson, Anthony K., author.
Title: Patrick Mahomes / by Anthony K. Hewson
Description: Minneapolis, Minnesota: Abdo Publishing Company, 2024 | Series: SportsZone biographies | Includes online resources and index.
Identifiers: ISBN 9781098291709 (lib. bdg.) | ISBN 9781098278250 (ebook)
Subjects: LCSH: Mahomes, Patrick, 1995--Juvenile literature. | Football players-- Biography--Juvenile literature. | Quarterbacks (Football)--Biography--Juvenile literature. | Professional athletes--Biography--Juvenile literature.
Classification: DDC 796.092--dc23

TABLE OF CONTENTS

Chapter One

MULTIPLE TALENTS

Patrick Mahomes's right ankle was throbbing as he dropped back to pass. There were just under three minutes to play in Super Bowl LVII on February 12, 2023. His Kansas City Chiefs were tied 35–35 with the Philadelphia Eagles. As he had done so many times before, Mahomes was trying to lead a game-winning drive.

It was first-and-10 for Kansas City at the Philadelphia 43-yard line. As Mahomes scanned the field for his receivers, he was suddenly swarmed by pass rushers. The Chiefs' star quarterback had been playing on an injured ankle for three games. But he had no choice. Mahomes had to run.

Spotting an open space up the middle of the field, Mahomes took off. To anyone watching, he clearly wasn't running full speed. Normally a graceful, athletic quarterback, Mahomes was laboring down the field. But he gritted his

Patrick Mahomes looks to pass during the second half of Super Bowl LVII.

FAST FACT

Patrick Mahomes and Philadelphia Eagles starting quarterback Jalen Hurts made history at Super Bowl LVII. It was the first time that two Black quarterbacks had ever started in the same Super Bowl.

teeth and managed to stay ahead of the chasing Philadelphia defenders. By the time he was caught by Eagles safety Kyzir White, Mahomes had gained 26 yards.

The gutsy effort helped set up Kansas City's go-ahead field goal with 11 seconds left to play. The team then held on to win 38–35 for its second Super Bowl in four years. It was proof that, even on one good leg, Mahomes was capable of greatness.

FROM PITCHER TO QUARTERBACK

Athletic excellence ran in the Mahomes family. Mahomes's father Pat was a Major League Baseball pitcher. When Patrick was born in 1995, his father was in his eighth of 22 professional seasons in the major and minor leagues. Though Patrick grew up in Texas, he spent a lot of time wherever his father was playing.

By the time he reached high school, Patrick was a star in baseball and basketball, in addition to football. He was even drafted by the Detroit Tigers baseball team after his senior season in 2014. But that same school year, he was also the Texas football player of the year. Patrick chose not to sign with the Tigers.

He instead enrolled at Texas Tech University and played both sports. When Mahomes first got to Texas Tech, he was the backup quarterback. But when starter Davis Webb was injured, Mahomes

Five-year-old Patrick Mahomes chases down fly balls with New York Mets pitcher Mike Hampton during batting practice before a World Series game in 2000.

got the chance to start the last four games of his freshman season in 2014. He threw 14 touchdowns with just two interceptions. As a result, Mahomes was named the starting quarterback as a sophomore and threw for 36 touchdowns while rushing for 10 more.

By his junior season, Mahomes had given up baseball to focus solely on football. The result was a record-setting year for the Red Raiders. Mahomes led the nation with 5,052 passing yards and 53 total touchdowns. Against Oklahoma, he shattered the college record for total yards in a game with 819. After the season, Mahomes was named the winner of the Sammy Baugh Trophy as the best passer in college football. He had the option to return for one more season at Texas Tech. But Mahomes felt he was ready for the National Football League (NFL).

Mahomes left Texas Tech with the third-most passing yards and touchdowns in team history.

Chapter Two

FROM BACKUP TO MVP

Despite Patrick Mahomes's record-setting numbers at Texas Tech, not everyone in the NFL thought he was ready for the professional game. The Red Raiders were known for passing the ball frequently. Several quarterbacks had put up huge numbers for the school. But none had succeeded in the NFL. Some scouts dismissed Mahomes as just another product of the Texas Tech system. Other teams thought Mahomes might need time to learn the complicated offenses of the NFL. They weren't about to spend a top pick on someone who could not play right away. But the Kansas City Chiefs didn't mind. They already had a good quarterback in Alex Smith. Mahomes could watch him from the bench and learn. Kansas City traded up in the draft to pick Mahomes 10th overall.

Mahomes calls out signals during his first preseason game for the Chiefs on August 11, 2017.

The Chiefs were already a good team. With Smith, Kansas City went 10–6 and won its division in 2017. The Chiefs had locked up their playoff spot with one game left, meaning Mahomes got the chance to see what he could do. He made his first NFL start on December 31, 2017, against the Denver Broncos.

Mahomes tossed a 51-yard pass to set up a touchdown on his first drive. He threw for 284 yards on the day, and Kansas City won 27–24. Though Mahomes did not throw any touchdown passes, he impressed onlookers by completing several tough throws.

GETTING HIS SHOT

The Chiefs traded Smith before the 2018 season and made Mahomes the starter. He did not disappoint. In the first game of the season, against the Los Angeles Chargers, Mahomes tossed four touchdown passes. In Week 2 against the Pittsburgh Steelers, Mahomes threw six more. No player had ever thrown 10 touchdowns in the first two weeks of a season.

Mahomes was beginning to make the teams that doubted him look foolish. He was also just getting warmed up. Those two

Mahomes's athletic ability helps him to attempt passes that few other NFL quarterbacks would even try.

games were the start of a magical, record-setting year. The Chiefs' record for touchdown passes in a season had been 30. Mahomes threw 31 in just 10 games. He ended up with 50 for the season. His 5,097 passing yards were also a team record.

Even more impressive than the numbers was how Mahomes played. Some of his passes were unlike anything NFL fans had ever seen. Mahomes hit receivers with sidearm and no-look passes. He threw accurate deep balls while defensive linemen were dragging him down. There was seemingly no throw he couldn't make.

In just one season, Mahomes had become the league's must-see quarterback. The Chiefs finished 12–4 and looked like Super Bowl contenders. Mahomes led them past the Indianapolis Colts in the divisional round, setting up a matchup with the New England Patriots in the American Football Conference (AFC) championship game. The Patriots were led by all-time great quarterback Tom Brady. The youngster and the legend put on a show. Mahomes threw three touchdown passes. He also led a four-play drive to set up a tying field goal in the final minute of the fourth quarter. But the Patriots got the ball first in overtime. Brady made sure the young phenom never saw the field. A 13-play touchdown drive won the game for New England, 37–31.

Mahomes didn't come away from the season empty-handed. He was honored as the NFL's Most Valuable Player (MVP). He was the first Chiefs player in history to win the award. And at 23, he was the NFL's youngest winner in more than 30 years.

Mahomes threw at least four touchdown passes in a game seven times during his MVP season in 2018.

Chapter Three

SIMPLY SUPER

E xcitement was high in Kansas City before the 2019 season. The Chiefs had the reigning MVP. And he had led them to within one win of the Super Bowl. Patrick Mahomes picked up right where he left off. Despite a nagging ankle injury picked up in a Week 1 win over the Jacksonville Jaguars, Mahomes piled up numbers while leading the Chiefs to a 4–2 start. But disaster struck in Week 7.

Facing the Denver Broncos on a Thursday night game, Mahomes went for a quarterback sneak near the goal line. He came out of the pile with a serious injury to his right knee. Immediately, fans, teammates, and even opponents feared Mahomes's injury would keep him out for a while. As he lay on the field, Broncos cornerback Chris Harris Jr. came over to shake Mahomes's hand and wish the popular quarterback well. "Hopefully he's not injured too bad, for the season," Harris said later. "He's great for our league."

Mahomes celebrates after throwing a touchdown pass against the Houston Texans early in the 2019 season.

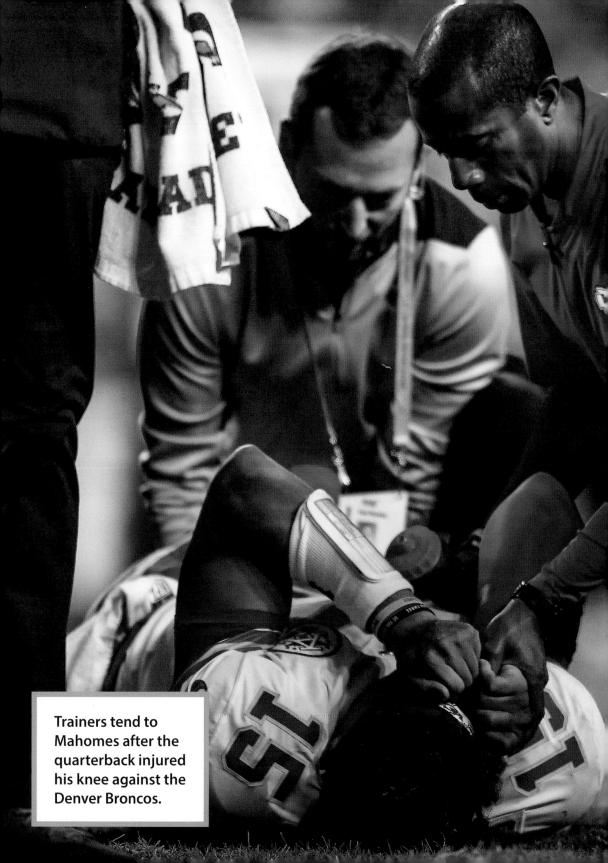

Trainers tend to Mahomes after the quarterback injured his knee against the Denver Broncos.

Mahomes had dislocated his kneecap. It was painful, but Kansas City breathed a sigh of relief when team doctors said he could be back in a month. Instead, Mahomes came back just three weeks later. His knee and ankle were both healed, and he threw for 446 yards and three touchdowns. However, the Chiefs lost 35–32 to the Tennessee Titans.

CHASING GREATNESS

Mahomes bounced back and led the team to a 6–0 finish and a 12–4 record overall. His personal numbers were not as strong due to the injuries, but he still threw for more than 4,000 yards with 26 touchdowns. Even better, the Chiefs looked ready for another deep playoff run.

Instead, they appeared to be on their way out of the playoffs before halftime of their first game. The Houston Texans raced out to a 24–0 lead. Mahomes stalked the sidelines, telling his teammates to "do something special." The star quarterback backed up his talk. With 9:55 left in the first half, Mahomes hit running back Damian Williams on a 17-yard

FAST FACT

As a kid Mahomes liked to eat ketchup sandwiches— bread, ketchup, and nothing else. Mahomes doesn't eat those anymore, but he still loves ketchup and earned an endorsement deal with the Hunt's brand in 2018.

touchdown pass. The Chiefs quickly got the ball back. On the next drive, Mahomes tossed a five-yard strike to tight end Travis Kelce with 8:05 left. And after the Texans fumbled the following kickoff return, the Chiefs' offense took the field full of confidence. Less than two minutes later, Mahomes hit Kelce again and it was 24–21. That pair connected for a third time with 44 seconds left in the half to give Kansas City the lead, 28–24. Kansas City scored on its first three drives of the second half as well as the Chiefs cruised to a 51–31 win.

Kansas City then faced the Titans in the AFC title game. Once again it looked like Tennessee would get the better of Mahomes. The Titans went up 17–7 early. But Mahomes went to work again. A touchdown pass to wide receiver Tyreek Hill cut the deficit to 17–14, and the Chiefs got the ball back before halftime. Mahomes led them down the field to the Tennessee 27-yard line, and with 23 seconds left, he scrambled to his left. After breaking two tackles in the backfield, he took off down the sideline. Mahomes then shook two more tacklers inside the 10 and fell into the end zone.

Mahomes gets a pass away under pressure during the Chiefs' playoff victory over the Houston Texans in the divisional playoffs on January 12, 2020.

Mahomes celebrates with teammate Frank Clark after Kansas City's victory in Super Bowl LIV on February 2, 2020.

The Chiefs went to the locker room with the lead again. Kansas City pulled away for a 35–24 win and a trip to the Super Bowl.

Mahomes's comeback abilities were on display again in the Super Bowl against the San Francisco 49ers. The Chiefs were down 20–10 with just over seven minutes left. Even worse, Kansas City faced third-and-15 from its own 35-yard line. During a timeout, Mahomes lobbied head coach Andy Reid and offensive coordinator Eric Bieniemy to let the quarterback air it out. Both coaches listened.

Mahomes dropped back to pass from the shotgun formation. A heavy San Francisco pass rush was on him. But just as he was hit, Mahomes launched a 44-yard bomb to Hill. A few plays later, Mahomes hit Kelce on a one-yard touchdown toss. Now it was 20–17 with 6:13 left to play.

The Chiefs quickly got the ball back. Seven plays later, Mahomes hit Williams on a five-yard touchdown pass. Kansas City had the lead and never looked back. Another touchdown on the Chiefs' next drive made it 31–20. The Chiefs' title was the team's first in a half century. After the game, Mahomes was named Super Bowl MVP. He had already given Kansas City fans a lifetime of memories, and he was still only 24.

Chapter Four

FRANCHISE QUARTERBACK

In 2020 the Kansas City Chiefs set out to give Patrick Mahomes a contract that would keep him around a long time. The Chiefs signed Mahomes to a new 10-year deal before the season worth up to $503 million. It showed just how special the Chiefs thought their leader and quarterback was.

Mahomes showed that leadership extended beyond the playing field in the summer of 2020. After the murder of George Floyd by police officers in Minneapolis, Mahomes joined several other NFL players in a video asking the NFL to work harder on encouraging racial dialogue in America. Many praised him for his stance. Former NFL receiver Anquan Boldin highlighted Mahomes's presence because the quarterback was such an important player. "A quarterback's voice carries," Boldin said.

Patrick Mahomes is introduced to the crowd in Kansas City before the AFC championship game on January 19, 2020.

On the field, Mahomes started 2020 with more comeback victories. In Week 2, Kansas City fell behind the Los Angeles Chargers 17–6 in the third quarter. Mahomes led a rally, even throwing a 54-yard touchdown pass. Kansas City won 23–20 in overtime. It was Mahomes's sixth win in a row after trailing by double figures. That was an NFL record.

The following week, on Monday night against the Baltimore Ravens, Mahomes surpassed 10,000 career passing yards. He had done it in 34 games, faster than any other NFL quarterback. He continued to roll, and so did the Chiefs. Kansas City finished the year 14–2.

Kansas City squeaked past the Cleveland Browns 22–17 in the divisional round of the playoffs. But Mahomes left the game with a concussion. No one was sure if he could play in the AFC championship against the Buffalo Bills. Mahomes passed the league's concussion tests during the week, then led another comeback win. Down 9–0 early, Mahomes threw for 325 yards and three touchdowns in a 38–24 victory.

Facing the Tampa Bay Buccaneers in the Super Bowl,

FAST FACT

Mahomes proposed to his girlfriend Brittany Matthews on the day the Chiefs received their Super Bowl rings in 2019. Mahomes and Matthews had been dating since high school. They had their first child in 2021, and the two were married in 2022.

Mahomes had a rare bad game. He threw two interceptions. The Chiefs were routed 31–9. Mahomes had to watch Tom Brady, who had joined Tampa Bay from New England before the season, celebrate a record sixth title.

GUTTING IT OUT

Mahomes led the Chiefs back to the AFC Championship Game for the fourth straight year in January 2022. However, the Chiefs lost 27–24 to the Cincinnati Bengals.

The next season, Mahomes came out slinging. He finished the year a career-high 5,250 passing yards and an NFL-best 41 touchdowns. Mahomes cruised to another league MVP Award.

Mahomes tries to get a pass away while being hit during Super Bowl LV in February 2021. The Tampa Bay Buccaneers sacked him three times in the game.

Mahomes explained his ability to stay calm during tense, high-scoring games in a text message to his former college coach, Kliff Kingsbury. After Mahomes beat the Pittsburgh Steelers 42–37 early in the 2018 season, Kingsbury told reporters that Mahomes wrote to him and said, "Coach, you know I don't blink in a shootout."

However, disaster struck in the team's first playoff game. Mahomes suffered a high ankle sprain in the second quarter after being pulled down by a Jacksonville Jaguars defender. He missed the rest of the first half while his ankle was X-rayed. But he refused to stay on the sidelines.

Mahomes returned in the second half and led two scoring drives in a 27–20 victory. But his status for the AFC Championship Game was a worry all week for Chiefs fans. Sure enough, Mahomes shook off the pain and played. He threw for 326 yards and two touchdowns. The Chiefs avenged their 2022 playoff loss to the Bengals by winning 23–20.

Even with two weeks between that game and the Super Bowl, Mahomes's ankle still wasn't fully healed. And he reinjured it on a play late in the second quarter against the Eagles. Kansas City fans had two reasons to worry as the team went into halftime trailing 24–14.

Once again, Mahomes bounced back. He threw two touchdown passes early in the fourth quarter to put Kansas City up 35–27. Then the Eagles marched down the field to tie the game.

But led by Mahomes's gusty scramble, Kansas City put kicker Harrison Butker in position to go ahead with 11 seconds left.

The kicker split the uprights. After the Eagles' desperation play failed on the final down, Mahomes was a champion again. After leading a second Super Bowl comeback, Mahomes was named the game's MVP. There could no longer be any doubt that he was one of the best quarterbacks the NFL had ever seen.

Mahomes celebrates after the Chiefs defeated the Philadelphia Eagles 38–35 in Super Bowl LVII.

GLOSSARY

concussion
A brain injury caused by a blow to the head or a violent shaking of the head and body.

contender
A person or team that has a good chance at winning a championship.

contract
An agreement to play for a certain team.

division
A group of teams that helps form a league.

draft
A system that allows teams to acquire new players coming into a league.

endorsement
When an athlete promotes a company in exchange for their products or money.

high ankle sprain
An injury that occurs when the ligaments that connect the ankle tendon to the shin bones become stretched or torn.

offensive coordinator
A football coach who is in charge of the team's offense and who often calls each play.

professional
A person who gets paid to perform.

sidearm
Throwing a ball off to the side of one's body as opposed to over the top.

MORE INFORMATION

BOOKS

Graves, Will. *GOATs of Football*. Minneapolis, MN: Abdo Publishing, 2022.

Hanlon, Luke. *Tom Brady*. Minneapolis, MN: Abdo Publishing, 2024.

Hewson, Anthony K. *Josh Allen*. Minneapolis, MN: Abdo Publishing, 2024.

ONLINE RESOURCES

To learn more about Patrick Mahomes, please visit abdobooklinks.com or scan this QR code. These links are routinely monitored and updated to provide the most current information available.

INDEX

ABOUT THE AUTHOR

Anthony K. Hewson is a freelance writer originally from San Diego. He and his wife now live in the San Francisco Bay Area with their two dogs.